# ULTIMATE

# FIELD TRIP 1

## ADVENTURES IN THE AMAZON RAIN FOREST

by Susan E. Goodman    photographs by Michael J. Doolittle

# ULTIMATE
# FIELD TRIP

## ADVENTURES IN THE AMAZON RAIN FOREST

by Susan E. Goodman     photographs by Michael J. Doolittle

ALADDIN PAPERBACKS

TO MATTHEW, MY FIRST READER, JACOB, MY CURRENT ONE,
AND TO ZACH WHO HAS ALWAYS BEEN THERE      —S. G.

TO AMITY      —M. D.

First Aladdin Paperbacks edition August 1999
Previously published as *Bats, Bugs, and Biodiversity: Adventures in the Amazonian Rain Forest* by Atheneum Books for Young Readers.
Text copyright © 1995 by Susan E. Goodman
Illustrations copyright © 1995 by Michael J. Doolittle
Aladdin Paperbacks, an imprint of Simon & Schuster Children's Publishing Division, 1230 Avenue of the Americas, New York, NY 10020
Also available in an Atheneum Books for Young Readers hardcover edition.
Book design by Anne Scatto/PIXEL PRESS
The text of this book was set in Fournier.
Printed and bound in Hong Kong
10   9   8   7   6   5   4   3   2
The Library of Congress has cataloged the hardcover edition as follows:
Goodman, Susan.
Bats, bugs, and biodiversity: adventures in the Amazonian rain forest / by Susan Goodman; photographs by Michael J. Doolittle.
p.   cm.
Includes bibliographical references
ISBN 0-689-31943-6
1. Rain forest ecology—Amazon River Region—Juvenile literature.
[1. Rain forest ecology—Amazon River Region.   2. Ecology—Amazon River Region.]   I. Doolittle, Michael, J., ill.   II. Title.
QH112.G66   1995   508.315'2'098543-dc20   94-35029
ISBN 0-689-82870-5 (Aladdin pbk.)

We would like to thank the following people for all their help and support of this project: Jim and Ruth Cronk (thanks guys!), Terry and Doug Larkin and the rest of the teachers and organizers from the Children's Environmental Trust Foundation; Richard Ryel and Dick Mills of International Expeditions; Peter Jenson and Pam Bucur of Explorama Lodge; Paul Donahue, Teresa Wood, Morgan Smith and all the other instructors at the workshop. Thanks to the extraordinary kids who opened their journals to us, especially our Morpho Blues who patiently posed with frogs and answered all our questions.

Thanks to readers Deborah Hirschland, Marjorie Waters, Carol Magun, and Doris Seale; and, to Dr. Gary Hartshorn of the World Wildlife Fund and Lynne Hartshorn for their excellent technical review of the manuscript.

A special thanks to Marcia Marshall who has been a great help every step of the way.

# Contents

# CHAPTER I

# THE ADVENTURE BEGINS

*"I'm so excited! We've been working for a year and, all of the sudden, we're almost there. It's just so Amaz(on)ing!"*
MARY RAIKES

For nearly a year, seventy-four seventh- and eighth-graders from western Michigan read, lived, and dreamed rain forest. They were part of a program called, "Rain Forest '93: A Children's Rain Forest Workshop," and their year of learning and earning money was capped off by a week's trip to the Peruvian Amazon.

Equipped with their journals, mosquito repellent, and stashes of candy, the group marched into their plane at the Miami airport. They buckled their seat belts and took off for a different world. A world where the exotic animals they'd only seen in zoos and picture books live in their natural habitat. A world where more species of ants crawl upon a single tree than can be found in all of Great Britain. A world disappearing so rapidly it might not exist when their children are ready to make the same trip.

The kids were divided into small groups. Here are the "Morpho Blues," named for a rain forest butterfly (from left to right): Emily DeKock, Taylor Campbell, Rebecca Howard, Dan Van Voorst, Annette Pak, Eme Slagh, Sara Torrey, Dan Huyser, Doug Boyer.

Despite all their studying, the kids were still filled with questions:

"Will I be able to say enough Spanish for people to understand me?"

"How do Indians get the poison from poison arrow frogs?"

"Will I ever get over my bug phobia?"

"Does anything eat tarantulas?"

"What will people think of me if I'm scared?"

3

Local teens dressed up in these traditional grass skirts and neckpieces to provide a special welcome.

# CHAPTER 2

# A First Look at Peru

Walking off the plane in Iquitos, the kids were greeted first with a blast of warm, wet air, then by the call of drums and wooden flutes. Suddenly, local teens danced up through the darkness. Their smiles and flying feet welcomed the group to Peru. A dancer held out a hand to his audience. One North American joined in, then another. Soon backpacks and cameras lay on the runway as everyone snaked and twirled to the music.

"You were with people who don't speak your language," said Taylor, "and it was fun to know you can become friends by dancing together. One girl took off her belt and just put it around my waist."

"As you're dancing, it hits you," added Annette, *"I'm in Peru!"*

The next morning, the group walked around Iquitos. On their tour, they dodged the motorized rickshaws that are used as taxis. They saw run-down tiled buildings that were once beautiful when Iquitos was rich from the sale of rain forest rubber. Their guide, Luis, also showed them a "floating village," where people from the jungle have set up houses on stilts at the edge of the Amazon. Here, like most places on the river, babies have swollen bellies from drinking river water containing parasites.

None of the kids had ever seen people living this way. "You realize how much you take for granted," said Rebecca. "There I was complaining about air-conditioning and I see a little kid sleeping in a house without walls."

"The books say this is a third world country," Sara added, "but we didn't really know what that means."

In the marketplace, they saw the many things people harvest from the jungle to sell in town. Some ribereños, or river people, had paddled hours in their dugout canoes to sell the charcoal they made by burning wood. Others brought plants used for medicine, fruits, and live animals such as ducks and land turtles to be cooked and eaten.

"Well, it's different," said Sara, tasting her first sip from a coconut.

"I like Sprite better," mumbled the next kid who tried it.

5

Some people travel a whole day, paddling heavy loads in their boats, to get to the Iquitos market.

"Hey, I did a report on that animal in school," called Dan when he spotted a three-toed sloth slowly climbing across a Peruvian's shoulders. As the group petted the animal, Luis learned that its mother had already been killed for food and this baby was to be sold as someone's dinner. The group decided to buy the sloth and return him to the rain forest. The sloth latched on to Luis's shoulder, so someone promptly named him "Static Cling."

Later, when he heard about the purchase, an instructor pointed out that saving the animal was not as simple as it first seemed. "You know the sloth is going to die if it stays in the market to be sold," he said. "But it might also die if you put it back in the forest, because it's too young to live on its own. And, by buying the sloth to save it, you may be encouraging the seller to trap more to sell to 'softhearted' eco-tourists.

"These are hard decisions," he continued, "but we have to think about the message we send with our dollars."

The kids wondered if there even was a right answer. "Maybe we should have explained our views to the guy," said Rebecca.

Once he heard that many local people hunt the jungle for the food on their table, Doug said, "People need money—and food—to live. So maybe they wouldn't care about what we were saying."

"Hey," said Abby. "Someone was going to buy it anyway. At least we saved one."

Sloths move so slowly, they can take more than a day to move from one tree to another.

"I keep thinking I'm on the 'Jungle Cruise' at Disney World. I can't believe this is not a dreamworld." **STEVE RYPMA**

# CHAPTER 3

# A Trip Down the Amazon

The ride downriver takes about three and a half hours.

**N**ext stop: Explorama Lodge, the group's jungle home, fifty miles down the Amazon by riverboat. To some kids, the *Amazon Queen*'s most interesting feature was her thatched roof. To others, it was her toilet, a seat over a hole in the boat, set apart in a tiny cabin.

"It's always flushing," said one boy, looking through the hole to the Amazon churning underneath.

"Just think of it as our way to contribute to this great waterway," said another as he closed the door behind him.

A look at life on the passing shore showed that the Amazon was not only its people's highway, but also their supermarket, their bathtub and washing machine, their kitchen sink and swimming hole. Men were fishing from dugout canoes. Women were washing clothes. Children were toting water, washing up, and splashing around for fun.

Years ago, the kids could have cruised for miles without seeing many houses on shore. Today, more and more people live along the Amazon and its tributaries. Traditionally, parents had a dozen or more children although often only two to four survived to adulthood. Medical care is still scarce, but the small amount now available helps more children live long enough to have children of their own. In addition, many Peruvians, unable to find work in the cities, have moved to make a new start in the jungle.

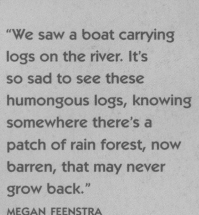

"We saw a boat carrying logs on the river. It's so sad to see these humongous logs, knowing somewhere there's a patch of rain forest, now barren, that may never grow back."
MEGAN FEENSTRA

9

# The Amazon River

How can you describe this river that starts with melting snow from the Andes Mountains and has arms reaching through nine countries to drain mist and rain from the world's largest jungle into the Atlantic Ocean?

It's big. It's the longest river in the world, sometimes deep enough to cover a ten-story building and, during the rainy season, up to twenty miles wide.

It's beyond big. One of its islands is larger than Vermont and Connecticut combined.

As one kid said, "It's totally awesome." Over two-thirds of the world's freshwater is found within its basin. In fact, the water pouring from the Amazon into the Atlantic each day would satisfy New York City's freshwater needs for nine years.

# CHAPTER 4

# SETTING UP BASE CAMP

"You'll notice big jugs all over the camp," announced a teacher. "These are filled with *gringo* (translation: North American) water, purified water for drinking and brushing your teeth. The pitchers of water in your rooms are for washing only. When you're finished, throw the dirty water out your window into the jungle.

"But," she said, "look to see who's out there before you do."

Tossing that water was easy enough; Explorama's bedroom windows contained no glass. Things should be as open as possible in a tropical rain forest so they have a chance to dry out. One hundred inches of rain a year put a lot of moisture

"I was scared to death to go to sleep for fear that a tarantula would get in my bed Do you think that's possible?"
ALLISON HEYNS
*(Mosquito netting keeps out more than mosquitoes!)*

in the air. It is so humid that washed socks take days to dry, eyeglasses and camera lenses fog up constantly, and postage stamps—not layered in wax paper—fuse into a useless lump.

With open bedrooms, a screened-in dining room, and hammocks everywhere, the kids were never shut off from nature. Their alarm clocks and lullabies were the sounds of frogs, birds, and insects protecting territories or looking for love. "I never thought I could hear so many sounds," said one girl. "They make you feel like you're in prehistoric times."

"You can hear a thousand sounds but not see a single sign of insects or animals," observed another.

In fact, some kids felt disappointed at first by the rain forest's seemingly empty sea of green. "I thought there would be more animals," was Rebecca's initial reaction. But the kids soon learned creatures stay alive by staying hidden. With practice, they saw that that dried bunch of leaves was actually a sloth high in a cecropia tree, that twig was an insect known as a walking stick, and that roll of leaves revealed the leg of a tarantula waiting for her nightly prowl. Four square miles of rain forest typically have 125 species of animals, 400 of birds, 100 of reptiles, 60 of amphibians, 150 of butterflies, and maybe more than 40,000 species of other insects.

12

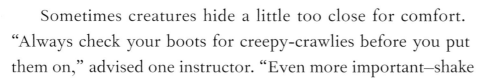

Sometimes creatures hide a little too close for comfort. "Always check your boots for creepy-crawlies before you put them on," advised one instructor. "Even more important—shake out your underwear each morning."

The kids had their first encounter with "solar-heated" showers (showers that used cool river water warmed by a little sunshine) and kerosene lamps lighting the night inside and out. Their outhouse bathrooms were shared with moths, katydids, and who knows what. Foods like *yuca* and *plantains* were on their meal trays along with juice made from fruits they had never seen before. There were so many things to get used to, even before they set foot on a jungle trail.

"I'm getting used to not having electricity. If you think about it, we really could get along without it."
SARA TORREY

"Don't bypass any experience here that is safe," advised instructor Morgan Smith. "This is the chance of a lifetime. Drink it, eat it, live it."

And they did. In the week that followed, the kids took workshops on everything from bugs and birds to bats and biodiversity. They climbed into the treetops, trampled through mud, swung on vines, and paddled canoes. At Explorama and the other camps farther downriver, they studied the world's greatest living laboratory—the Amazon rain forest.

13

# CHAPTER 5

# UP IN THE CANOPY

The jungle canopy is one of the earth's last unexplored frontiers. Scientists who had studied species within reach already knew that tropical rain forests are our planet's richest ecosystem. Until recently they had no idea that, over their heads, an amazing number of unknown plants and animals was living and dying without ever coming down to earth.

One entomologist, for example, sprayed several rain forest trees to strip them of all their insects. Approximately 80 percent—four out of five—of the insects he found were new species.

So the kids felt like pioneers when they stepped out on the only canopy walkway in the Amazon. Starting from a platform built around the trunk of a 150-foot shimbillo tree, they set off on a narrow bridge that slanted upward to the second giant tree. They zigzagged from one huge tree to the next, up and up again, until they got a true bird's-eye view of the canopy.

"We're so high but I'm not even scared," said Doug looking down eighty feet to the ground.

"The canopy walkway was fun, exciting, wonderful, scary, frightening and every other word you can use that describes your mixed feelings."
SARA TORREY

"Oh yeah?" answered a friend. "I'm having a massive sweat attack." A sweat attack was a small price to pay for a trip to this fantastic treetop world bursting with life. Fed by the tremendous energy of the tropical sun, the canopy is a factory where 90 percent of the jungle's photosynthesis takes place, using the sunlight to create food for its plants. Here, epiphytes, plants that live on trees without harming them, park themselves in the light. Lianas, or vines, hitch a ride toward the sun. More than fifty different plant species can attach themselves to one tree. These plants flower and fruit, providing food for insects, birds, and larger animals—who, in turn, are food for different insects, birds, and larger animals.

15

"That bird looks like someone colored it with a crayon," said Doug, pointing out a bright aqua spangled cotinga.

"These look like giant versions of our houseplants at home," said Dan, looking at the philodendron vine with leaves four feet long.

Some kids thought the view from the last platform, 118 feet high, was the most spectacular part of the day. "When you look out over the trees, it's like you can see to the ends of the earth," one observed. "Being up there makes you talk in a whisper."

Others preferred their chance to perch in the trees like a monkey or macaw. Any kid who wanted to could

inch up a rope into a nearby emergent, take a look around, then slide down another rope to the forest floor far below. Although mountaineering equipment made the whole thing safe, "it was really frightening," said a climber. "But I didn't even notice because I was having so much fun."

"An indescribable moment is when you descend from the canopy into the understory, looking at all that empty space," added another. "Your heart beats triple time. Afterward I danced all the way back to the lodge!"

Dylan slides down a rope to the forest floor after visiting the treetop world of the canopy walkway.

# Strata of the Rain Forest

Each layer of the rain forest captures light and heat from above while trapping humidity below. As a result, each layer has its own unique environment inhabited by different kinds of life.

The CANOPY, the rain forest's dense ceiling, is made of trees over sixty-five feet high. These trees grow straight and tall, putting out branches once they reach the sun. Popping through the canopy here and there is the emergent layer, trees 130 feet or higher. Fully exposed to sun and wind, this layer endures temperatures of 90 degrees or more, but only about 60 percent humidity.

The UNDERSTORY, from near ground level to the canopy, consists of shrubs, smaller trees, and young canopy trees pushing toward the light. Many of its plants and trees have larger leaves than those living in the canopy, so they can absorb as much of the dim light as possible.

Only 1 to 2 percent of the sun's light ever reaches the rain forest FLOOR. Its few plants have thin, very large leaves to absorb what light is available. Its average humidity

of 90 percent, however, is perfect for the fungi and bacteria that team up with termites and earthworms to decompose, break down, the dead plants and animals that drop here. The forest, thirsty for nourishment, quickly reabsorbs the nutrients from them. Shallow tree roots take up these nutrients; some insects lay eggs on dead animals to provide their offspring with a ready food supply. So few nutrients are left in the soil that the rain forest has been called the "wet desert."

# Life in the Canopy

By flashing "fake eyes" on the underside of its wings, this owl butterfly may fool a predator into thinking it too is being chased. This may give the butterfly the time it needs to escape.

By blending in with its background, this gecko avoids being seen by predators.

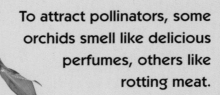

To attract pollinators, some orchids smell like delicious perfumes, others like rotting meat.

The toucan's bill is surprisingly lightweight and helps the bird clip fruit from branch tips.

Getting water in the canopy can be a problem. Some epiphytes, called bromeliads, form a tank with their leaves to store water. The tanks also collect leaves and insects, which decompose in them and provide nutrients. Monkeys drink from these "sky ponds"; birds hunt insects there. This tree frog lays its eggs in "tank" bromeliads.

This dead-leaf mimic katydid's camouflage comes from looking like its surroundings. The forest is full of insects posing as twigs, leaves, even bird droppings.

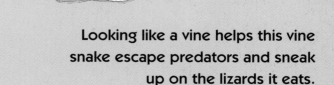

Looking like a vine helps this vine snake escape predators and sneak up on the lizards it eats.

Night monkeys are nocturnal; their large eyes have special features that help them use the night's dim light.

# CHAPTER 6

# THE SCHOOL VISIT

"*Bienvenidos a nuestros visitantes que vinieron de muy lejos.* . . . Welcome to our visitors who came from very far away," the mayor said in Spanish, his speech translated for his guests from Michigan. "This is the first time we have had a visit such as this one. This community is many families that feel as one family and that family welcomes you."

When the kids went to visit the schoolchildren of the town of Sapo Playa, they were surprised to see the entire community gathered to greet them. "This was a big event," commented Taylor.

"My partner's name was Margarita. I asked her how many people were in her family and she said nine. Wow, that's a lot."
TAYLOR CAMPBELL

The game called "duck, duck, goose" in the United States is named *"hola, hola, adiós"* (translation: hello, hello, good-bye) in Peru.

"Having all the families there made me feel welcome," said Annette. "It didn't matter that I couldn't always understand what they were saying."

During the day, the visitors noticed differences between them and their hosts. Size was one. "The children there were about half my size and most were older than me," remarked one boy.

Schooling was another. Some students walked a half hour through the jungle, others paddled an hour in a dugout to get to their one-room school. Two teachers taught the only six grades offered locally. Sometimes these grades took years to complete because kids left school to help their parents farm, fish, and mind younger brothers and sisters.

But the visitors also noticed important similarities. "The kids down there are like us," said Rebecca. "We all like having fun."

All day long the Peruvians and North Americans enjoyed their similarities, using music and sports as their common

In summer, the water level of the Amazon starts to go down. A bridge made from dugouts helped the group cross the mud to their boat.

23

language. They serenaded each other with songs, one group accompanied by wooden flutes, the other by kazoos. They partnered up for sack and canoe races.

Then they exchanged gifts. In moments, Peruvians were using their new U.S. maps to see where their guests had come from. They were trying out strange things called Frisbees. North Americans were admiring gifts made by their hosts. Some held carved toucans or turtles, others woven baskets and fans.

"My partner gave me a small wooden canoe he had carved himself," said one girl. "I like it a lot because he took the time to build it—that's what made it precious."

On the boat back from Sapo Playa, Sara tried to imagine the Peruvian children's reaction to her school in Michigan. "I think they might be overwhelmed," she said. "They might think it's really neat but then they would want to come home. Because home is wherever you're used to."

"When we got back, I walked to the showers. I was covered with a layer of mud so I didn't bother taking off my clothes or shoes."

TIM TATTAN

# Pressures on the Rain Forest

People throughout the Amazon are chopping down the rain forest to sell its lumber. They are chopping it down to farm although, in many areas, the soil is too poor to produce crops for more than a few years. They are chopping it down for cattle pastures but, again, the soil is so poor that each square yard only produces enough beef for three Quarter Pounders before it's abandoned. By the year 2000, half the world's tropical rain forests will no longer exist as rain forests.

The world needs the rain forest to help clean the air we breathe and make the medicines that keep us well. But the people who live in rain forests have needs too. So when Eme asked, "Do these people know what they are doing to the rain forest?" a teacher answered with another question: "If you had to choose between chopping down some trees and feeding your family, what would *you* do?"

25

# CHAPTER 7

# A Walk in the Jungle

"**M**ovies show people fighting the jungle. That's ridiculous, you can't fight this," Morgan said, waving his hand toward a tangle of roots and vines so thick it would hide a trail just ten feet away. "To survive, you must respect the jungle. You must join with it."

H. Morgan Smith would know. He spent several years with the Choco Indians in the rain forest in Panama. For the past forty years, he has taught others how to stay alive in the jungle with

When the kids ate the white cover off these guava seeds, it tasted like vanilla ice cream and melted in their mouths.

little more than a machete and, of course, the most important survival tool.

"Your best survival kit is right between your ears," said Morgan. "It's common sense, a combination of education and experience. If you understand your environment, you can survive—and, the environment can survive also. If you know what's dangerous, you can relax and enjoy what's beautiful."

Within a few steps, Morgan began introducing the kids to the rain forest's secrets. He showed them its dangers—a dumbcane plant, for example, that, if bitten, could swell your tongue until you suffocate. He opened the jungle's medicine chest—bryophytes, mosslike plants that are used for soothing wounds, and ants with huge jaws that you can force to bite both sides of a bad cut. When you twist their bodies off, the ants' mandibles remain, acting like stitches to keep the gash closed.

Morgan showed them a jungle drinking fountain, cutting through a *bejuco de agua* (translation: water vine) that furnishes water to drink if you have none. If too much water was the problem, Morgan pointed out "nature's Styrofoam." The bumps on water hyacinths' leaf stems float so well that they keep the plant on top of the water. If enough of these stems were stuffed in your shirt, they could act as a life jacket to keep you on top of the water too.

"Respect the environment," said Morgan. "If you cut something down, plant two in its place."

Peel the bark of a balsa tree, then strip off the fiber that lines it. If you twist the lengths of fiber together, you can make a rope that supports 150 pounds or more.

Morgan's walk not only taught the kids how to save their lives in the jungle, but also how to live there. Learning how local people used the thorny root of the stilt palm as a food grater and the rough leaves of the *chumico* vine as sandpaper, the kids began to understand that these more "primitive" peoples have very sophisticated ways of tapping the rain forest's resources. And, unlike more "sophisticated" peoples, they often used the forest in ways that conserve it.

"Life out here is hard work," said Morgan. "If you don't believe me, just try to build a thatch-roofed house."

And so they did—at least they cut down palm leaves and split them, the first step in making a thatched roof that can shed the jungle's constant rainfall for up to eight years. When she'd

28

finished, Sara didn't know what to do with the used palm leaves. "Just put them down," said Morgan with a twinkle in his eye. "They are biodegradable."

After the kids split palms, tried the machete, and stripped balsa bark to make rope, they realized how much work and skill it takes to live off the land. Once they visited a *ribereño* family, they saw how different their lives would be if they grew up in the jungle. There they watched children, their age and much younger, demonstrate their daily chores—hulling rice, squeezing juice from sugarcane, peeling yuca roots, clearing land with a machete.

After they tried these chores themselves, most of the group couldn't believe how much responsibility the children had. Dan's reaction? "They are more equipped than us. We have all these conveniences but we wouldn't know what to do without them."

Annette said, "I would love to live in the rain forest and know all the things they do. But I don't think I would want to do all that work and go to the bathroom outside."

These mosquito-netted beds are at Napo, the smaller camp where Morgan led his workshop.

# Symbiotic Relationships

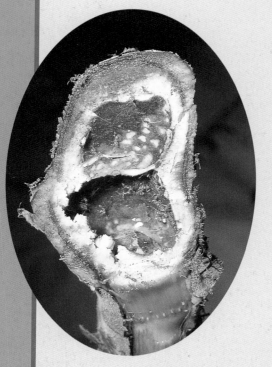

This cross-section of a cecropia branch shows the hollow spaces that are home to the Azteca ants.

Morgan also pointed out a cecropia tree. This tree teams up with Azteca ants to form a symbiotic relationship or partnership in which each member benefits. The cecropia's hollow trunk gives the ants a place to live. The tree also feeds the ants by producing a starchy food at the base of its leaf stalks. In return, the ants patrol the cecropia, stinging leaf-eating insects to drive them off, throwing sprouting epiphytes overboard, and cutting the tendrils of vines before they can attach.

The rain forest is full of such obliging partnerships. The sloth, for example, gives algae a home and consequently takes on a greenish tint, helpful camouflage in the treetops.

Actually, no jungle plant or animal lives a separate life. Each has adapted to take advantage of certain features of the jungle, like the hummingbird whose long beak can poke into trumpet-shaped flowers for nectar. Each has adapted to perform special tasks for others, like when that same hummingbird carries pollen from flower to flower in its search for food. These associations build upon one another to create the life of the rain forest (or any ecosystem, for that matter).

As one instructor said, "A bush is not just a separate thing. It gives shade to other plants, gets pollinated by birds, provides food for the fungi underneath, and so on."

# CHAPTER 8

# TRADING WITH THE YAGUA

The chief paints the kids' faces with *achiote*, a seed the Yagua use to decorate themselves.

"The Yagua still use their own language," explained our guide, Luis. "But in twenty years, they may not be here anymore."

For centuries, native Amazonian peoples had an unchanging life deep within the rain forest. They hunted monkeys, tapirs, and even toucans for meat. They gathered honey, fruits, and roots. Many tribes planted crops like yuca and yams, using slash-and-burn agriculture, a method that uses fire to clear patches of forest for a few years of farming. When these small plots are abandoned for more fertile ground, the forest has no problem growing back.

Modern times have threatened this native way of life. More than ninety Amazonian tribes have died out this century. Some groups have retreated into the jungle to maintain their customs. Others, like the Yagua, try to blend past and present.

"The Yagua used to be a fighting tribe," Luis said. "Now they seem to want to trade."

31

"The Indians definitely make beautiful things! Some jewelry has animal parts on it. If we took those, it would encourage the people to kill the animals. So we could just trade for things with seeds and beans."
APRIL WITTEVEEN

A seven-foot blowgun takes three weeks to make. Each dart is dipped in the poison curare before it is used to hunt birds and small animals.

Trading was the main attraction of the visit to a local Yagua Indian village. The kids were interested in the oval communal house the chief used for ceremonies. They were impressed with the blowgun demonstration when a man hit a small bundle of cigarettes from fifty feet away. But everyone was happiest when the trading began.

"At first it was difficult to just walk up to someone and ask for the headdress they were wearing," said Emily. "But, as time progressed, people were getting more and more daring. The Indians really like colorful T-shirts."

T-shirts topped the list of popular trading items. The Yagua also liked to bargain for running shorts, flip-flops, bandannas, fishing line and hooks, Tupperware, pocketknives, and pens, among other things. Sometimes they would accept amusements like barrettes or toys.

But not always. "I enjoyed seeing the Yagua laugh when I tried trading a troll," said one kid, who then pulled a T-shirt out of her backpack.

The trading continued. Four T-shirts for one blowgun, two T-shirts and a pair of running shorts for another. A comb for a necklace, a mirror and pen for a carved doll. Sara offered two hair bands for a carved canoe and the Yagua woman just ignored her. When one boy ran out of items to trade, he looked through his pack and found some dirty socks—which went quickly!

When Dan exhausted his trading supply, he pulled out his toothbrush and toothpaste. As he handed them over for two necklaces, he said, "We're only here for a few more days. I was hardly using them anyhow!"

33

# What the Rain Forest Means to Us

The list sounds like half the grocery store: coffee, bananas, cinnamon, rice, tea, lemons, oranges, pineapples, grapefruit, peanuts, sugar, chocolate. Many products we depend on come from the rain forest.

Not just food. And not just the rubber in our tires. Rain forest plants are the base of one quarter of our medicines—so far. Scientists have only studied one out of every one hundred rain forest plant species for medicinal value.

The rain forest affects the weather around the world. It absorbs huge amounts of energy

Originally from Africa and India, but now spread to tropics around the world, the rosy periwinkle is the source of some of our most effective anticancer drugs.

from the sun, but also manages to give a lot of it back. When rainfall is pumped back into the air through evaporation, it carries heat along with it. When trees give off moisture from the surface of their leaves, heat accompanies that water too. Winds then push the moisture and the warmth to cooler parts of the globe.

The rain forest is also a good weapon against global warming. Plants take carbon dioxide, a gas that adds to the greenhouse warming effect, from the air. In return, they release oxygen.

The United States and Europe used to be covered with great forests. They were chopped down to build farms, cities, and factories. Now the people in rain forest countries want lives as comfortable as ours. How can we expect these people, most of them poor, to make all the sacrifices necessary to protect their forests?

If rain forests benefit the entire world, perhaps the entire world should help support them. Some experts suggest finding less destructive ways to harvest rain forest lumber. Others suggest bringing renewable crops—Brazil nuts, nuts from the tagua palm to make buttons, unusual fruits such as guanabana, copaiba oil for hair conditioners—into the world market, where we can all help by buying them. Still others say we should support organizations that help pay off tropical countries' debts if they agree to protect rain forest land.

Yet, for any solution to succeed, it must take the needs and beliefs of rain forest people into account. As one instructor put it, "I don't think it's right for one culture to insist they have the answers for another. We can only hope that being aware and working for others' awareness can help."

35

**RIBBET RIBBET**
"Today we saw a frog bigger than my journal. Then it started raining and we cut some huge leaves off a tree to use as umbrellas."
REBECCA HOWARD

# CHAPTER 9

# OTHER NEAT STUFF

One evening, a boy wrote in his journal, "*Mucho* (translation: a lot) happened today." From bird-watching at sunrise to bat netting at nightfall, "*mucho*" happened each day the kids were in the rain forest. In workshops such as "Tropical Aquarium," they learned there are more fish species in the Amazon than in the entire Atlantic Ocean. In "The Corner Drugstore," a look at the jungle's medicinal plants, they learned that tea made from philodendron vines can treat a bite from the fer-de-lance, a poisonous snake.

They saw trees that avoid vines and epiphytes by shedding their bark every six months. They smelled orchids that fool male bees into pollinating them by masquerading as female bees. They heard about electric eels that generate 600 volts of current, enough to stun a horse. As one girl said, "What will this world think of next?"

The poison arrow frog's bright colors tell predators to stay away. Indians use a few species to poison darts for their blowguns. The "sweat" of one frog can coat as many as fifty darts.

Frogs can range from eight inches long to under an inch in length.

Termites live in large colonies in nests attached to trees. They eat wood and play an essential role in recycling nutrients.

## THE ANTS—AND OTHER BUGS— GO MARCHING

Blown up to human size, these leaf-cutting ants would be marching at fifteen miles per hour and carrying 750 pounds. Traveling in columns of ten thousand or more, these workers snip leaves and bring them back to colonies of up to 3 million. There, other workers mix the leaves with saliva and excrement to grow a fungus they feed to young ants. The ants eat only this fungus and this fungus is only found in leaf-cutting colonies—another example of symbiotic relationships.

## RAIN FOREST SCIENCE

A photometer measures light in units called foot-candles. The kids measured 1,650 foot-candles of light in open space, 75 in second growth forest, 18 in *virgin forest*. Measuring humidity, they found 56 percent humidity in open space, 75 percent in second growth forest, and 100 percent in the deepest jungle.

## TROPICAL AQUARIUM

"Lucio taught me to cast a net by holding some of it in my hands, over my elbow, on my wrist, and in my mouth. Then you give a big swing with your arms and let go of everything at once. If done correctly, the net spreads out, sinks, and captures everything inside."

SONJA HUEBNER

"I got pretty good with that cast-net. I caught a fish that's for sale in pet shops. It's weird to think that things natives catch right in their yards are for sale in the U.S."

APRIL WITTEVEEN

"I saw some lily pads that would probably hold 15 pounds! Each was over three feet in diameter. On the undersides were razor sharp spikes. Boy, would I hate to come up under one of those!"

TIM CHASE

# CHAPTER 10

# HOMEWARD BOUND

"It's already our last day here," said Emily. "I don't want to leave. I'm excited to see my family, but can't they come here instead?"

Many kids said they thought their trip to the rain forest had changed their lives. "I really think this trip has helped me be more aware of everything around me," said one girl. "You really learn how to use your eyes."

During this week, the group saw their studies come alive. Birds like toucans and macaws flew out of textbook illustrations and up into the forest canopy. A word like "biodiversity" became the swimming, growing, crawling life all around them each second they were in the jungle. An idea like extinction became painfully real as the kids saw more clearly what the world would lose.

They also learned that, like saving a sloth, preserving

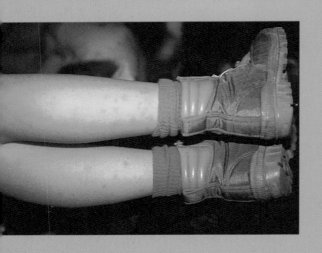

the rain forest is a lot more complicated than just saving trees. As Eme put it, "When you say 'rain forest,' most kids think about trees and animals, but you also have to think about people." For the first time, many of the group realized that any plans to save the rain forest must take into account the needs and dreams of the people who live there.

As they were preparing to leave, some kids were too busy stuffing muddy clothes into their duffel bags to do anything but try to figure out how to get a seven-foot blowgun onto the airplane. But other kids were already looking back. "I want to remember the clear sky at night where the stars appear close enough to touch."

Others were looking forward. "The first thing I'm going to do," said Rebecca, "is go to a real bathroom and get a pizza."

"I bet I'll forget to flush the toilet," added her friend, "because I'm so used to outhouses."

A few kids were looking beyond families and warm showers to telling others what they had learned. Their upcoming "year of advocacy" was as much a part of their program as the previous year of study and the week in Peru. Some of the students would talk to elementary schools and service clubs about their experiences. Others would make

40

posters for teachers or write letters to elected officials about rain forest issues.

What messages did they want to get across? "That Peruvians live there and it is their home," said one girl. "It's not really fair if we take away their stuff when we already have much more than them."

"I used to think, So what if trees are being cut down on the other side of the world, it doesn't affect me," added another. "Now I know that it does affect me and we can't sit back."

"I love the rain forest, absolutely love it. I mean, can you ever imagine a palm branch so big it takes three people to get across it? Or a colony of ants that go for miles just to carry pieces of leaves twice their size? Or an animal that moves so slowly it barely ever goes down the tree and has green stuff growing on its fur? Or, what about the fish that's as content to walk in the mud as it is to swim in the river? Or, a place that has so many different insects we haven't even identified them all yet?

Well, I can only think of one place where all these things are true—the rain forest. It just breaks my heart to think that my children may never get to see this place, only in pictures, as a part of history. We've got to save it before it's too late."

MEGAN FEENSTRA

# Glossary

BACTERIA—microscopic one-celled organisms that help break down dead materials into soil

BIODEGRADABLE—able to be broken down into soil by organisms like bacteria

BIODIVERSITY—the variety of living things

CANOPY WALKWAY—a system of bridges between trees that allows scientists to be high in the rain forest

COMMUNAL HOUSE—a larger hut used by an entire Indian village for ceremonies like marriage

DECOMPOSE—the process in which tiny living things, such as termites and bacteria, break down dead plants and animals into nutrients that can be used again to feed other life

DUGOUT CANOES—boats made by carving and hollowing out a log

ECO-TOURISTS—people who, when traveling, are concerned about preserving the environment

EMERGENT—a tree that is much taller than other trees in the canopy

ENTOMOLOGIST—a scientist who studies insects

EPIPHYTES—plants that live upon other plants without harming them

FUNGI—tiny organisms that break down and feed upon another—usually dead—organism

GREENHOUSE EFFECT—a gradual warming of the earth caused by the heat of gases trapped in the atmosphere

HABITAT—all aspects of a plant or animal's home, from its food and shelter to its protection from danger

HUMIDITY—amount of water in the air held as vapor

LIANAS—woody vines that twist up rain forest trees to get to the canopy

MACHETE—a large, heavy knife used for many things including chopping away the jungle's underbrush

MANDIBLES—an insect's "jaws" used for biting food or for defense

NOCTURNAL—occurring or active at night

NUTRIENTS—things used as food by plants and animals

PARASITES—organisms that live and feed on or in another organism without benefiting that host organism

PHOTOSYNTHESIS—the process plants use to turn the energy in sunlight, carbon dioxide, and water into food

PLANTAIN—a starchy fruit that looks like a banana and is a very important food in many tropical countries

POLLINATORS—insects, birds, and animals that transfer pollen from one flower to
    another
PREDATORS—plants or animals that hunt others for food
RIBEREÑOS—people who have adapted their lives to living on the river
SECOND GROWTH FOREST—the plants and trees that grow back once the original
    trees have been cut down, usually including thicker vegetation at the forest floor
SPECIES—a group of plants or animals that share common traits and can come
    together to reproduce
STILT PALM—a palm whose roots also grow above ground so the base of
    the trunk is in the air
SYMBIOTIC RELATIONSHIP—
    or mutualism, when two or more
    species form a partnership in which
    all benefit
VIRGIN FOREST—or primary forest, an
    undisturbed forest
YUCA—a starchy root, an important
    food source in tropical countries

Two kids try to make friends
with a capybara.

44

# Further Reading

## BOOKS FOR YOUNG PEOPLE

Aldis, Rodney. *Rainforests*. New York: Dillion Press, 1991.

Cherry, Lynne. *The Great Kapok Tree: A Tale of the Amazon Rain Forest*. San Diego: Harcourt Brace and Jovanovich, 1990.

Forsyth, Adrian. *Journey Through a Tropical Jungle*. New York: Simon & Schuster, 1988.

George, Jean Craighead. *One Day in the Tropical Rain Forest*. New York: Thomas Y. Crowell, 1990.

Goodman, Billy. *The Rain Forest*. New York: Tern Enterprise, Inc., 1991.

Miller, Christina G., and Louise A. Berry. *Jungle Rescue: Saving the New World Tropical Forest*. New York: Atheneum, 1991.

Zak, Monica. *Save My Rainforest*. Volcano, Calif: Volcano Press, 1992.

## OTHER BOOKS YOU MIGHT TRY

Collins, Mark, ed.. *The Last Rain Forests*. New York: Oxford University Press, 1990.

Forsyth, Adrian, and Ken Miyata. *Tropical Nature*. New York: Charles Scribner's Sons, 1984.

Lewis, Scott. *The Rainforest Book*. Los Angeles: Living Planet Press, 1990.

Mitchell, Andrew W. *The Enchanted Canopy*. New York: Macmillan, 1986.

# More Information About This Program

FOR MORE INFORMATION ABOUT THE CHILDREN'S RAIN FOREST WORKSHOPS PROGRAM, CONTACT:

Jim Cronk
Children's Environmental Trust Foundation, International
572 Alice Street
Zeeland, Michigan 49464
TEL: 1-616-772-7250

FOR MORE INFORMATION ABOUT OTHER RAIN FOREST WORKSHOPS FOR CHILDREN, CONTACT:

Veronica Rhoads
International Expeditions, Inc.
One Environs Park
Helena, Alabama 35080
TEL: 1-800-633-4734